French Enameled Ware
for the Collector

Yves Moureau
and
Elyan Reboul

4880 Lower Valley Road, Atglen, PA 19310 USA

Dedication

This book is dedicated to the love of French enameled ware
and to all the collectors.

Rare spice canister set, complete, six pieces with stylized raised floral design
and gothic lettering. *Courtesy of The French Corner.* $650-750.

Designed by Joseph M. Riggio Jr.
Type set in Bernhard Mod BT/Lydian BT

ISBN: 0-7643-1809-8
Printed in China
1 2 3 4

Published by Schiffer Publishing Ltd.
4880 Lower Valley Road
Atglen, PA 19310
Phone: (610) 593-1777; Fax: (610) 593-2002
E-mail: Info@schifferbooks.com
Please visit our web site catalog at www.schifferbooks.com
We are always looking for people to write books on new and related
subjects. If you have an idea for a book, please contact us at the
above address.

This book may be purchased from the publisher.
Include $3.95 for shipping.
Please try your bookstore first.
You may write for a free catalog.

In Europe, Schiffer books are distributed by
Bushwood Books
6 Marksbury Avenue
Kew Gardens
Surrey TW9 4JF England
Phone: 44 (0) 20 8392 8585
Fax: 44 (0) 20 8392 9876
E-mail: Bushwd@aol.com
Free postage in the UK. Europe: air mail at cost.

Contents

Charming blue coffee pot with filter, decorated with raised cherries. *Courtesy of The French Corner.* $350-420.

Pink coffee pot with hand painted flowers, 9" tall. *Courtesy of The French Corner.* $270-295.

Acknowledgments

Firstly, we would like to especially thank Tina Skinner of Schiffer Publishing for her help and for giving us the idea to write this book.

To all the antique show producers who trusted "The French Corner" by accepting us into their show four years ago – even if, at that time, a booth exclusively dedicated to French enameled ware could have appeared as before its time. Michael and Marilyn Grimes, for the Calendar antique show in Del Mar; Yvonne Bustamante, for the Bustamante antique show in Pasadena and Santa Monica; April Thede, for C.A.M.L's antique show in Santa Barbara; Bob Taylor, for Hillsborough antique show in San Mateo (San Francisco area); Chris Palmer, for Palmer-Wirfs antique show in Portland Oregon; John Sauls, for Marburger antique show in Round Top Texas; and recently, Bill Summers for his show in Ketchum, Sun Valley Idaho.

To all our friends in the United States, Bob Watson and Kathy Klingaman of Transatlantique, a special thanks to Kathy Sarr of Laura's Cottage, to our collector friends Adria Iwanyk and John Popko for sharing their pieces and passion with us.

In Europe, Ingrid and Christophe for helping us to find wonderful pieces, Veronique Besluau, Arlette, she will recognize herself, to all the persons who kindly kept pieces for us, and all our friends that support us morally and technically, Cathy Van Biesen and Mike. To Madame B. Droumaguet station manager in Paris of AOM now called Air Lib, and to all our ex-colleges.

And last but not the least, Mami in Belgium who is hunting successfully with tenacity and courage.

Unusual composition shows in the design of this coffee pot in raised enamel, with a fastened spout, c. 1880. *Courtesy of The French Corner.* $620-680.

Introduction

Several books have already been written on enameled ware. But we wanted this one to be different, to be a book based only on French enameled ware. We wanted to talk about art in general, instead of making this book very technical or scientific. Indeed, we believe that it is about time to consider enameled ware as real pieces of art and not only "kitchen stuff," as some people like to call it.

Certainly, we all know that primary artistic works create the strongest impressions, but art can also be found in more modest creations; often, it is even more heartwarming this way.

The time has come to realize that enameled ware can be seen as the reflection of a way of life – a certain art of manufacturing and the skills of dedicated workers from the nineteenth to the twentieth centuries. It is why we have to preserve it as witness to a particular era.

Now that you've caught a glimpse of our point of view, we would like to introduce you to the pieces featured in this book, which reflect many years of patience, research, and the happiness of finding a wonderful item…or more often, hoping to find one. Finding French enameled ware has indeed become more and more difficult than it used to be. Of course, we understand that the whole world is now collecting – indeed, the demand in Japan and the United States is tremendous! We also have to consider that Europe has been collecting for many years now, and the stock is therefore very limited. But, after all, isn't that the exciting and fun part of collecting?

The pieces shown in this book reflect, of course, our personal choice and taste. Nevertheless, we have tried our best to select pieces that are representative of a certain style, design, period, or – even if not decorated – are at least special by virtue of their shape.

We hope that this book will be enjoyable for both the novice and the knowledgeable, that it will inspire you to start your own collection, and that you will be touched, as we are, by the magic of French enameled ware.

Beautiful vegetable bucket with gold French lettering and garlands of roses. *Courtesy of The French Corner.* $650-680.

Chapter One

French or Not French?

Does French enameled ware really exist? Well...yes and no!

What we generally call French enameled ware should be considered, in fact, more as European enameled ware. The commonly used term "French enameled ware" should be understood as a generic term denoting a certain *style* of enameled ware, rather than a specific origin.

Of course, there *was* an important production of enameled ware in France – the most famous origin being the Japy-Frères company, whose pieces are highly collectible today. There were other companies in France as well, such as Luc, Émailleries du Loiret, Leopold, and Le Coq Gaulois, but it would be too restrictive to speak only about enameled ware actually produced in France.

The production, in fact, was all over Europe and extended even further out. Belgium created pieces of incredible quality, esthetically and technically; they came from companies with very famous names such as SAINT SERVAIS, Aubecq and CNEB. In Germany, names like Baumann (with a lion as symbol), Ullrich, and AnnWeiler are well known, while additional European manufacturers include Duco, Sphinx, and "B & B." Among the countries producing enameled ware are Austria, the former Czecho-

slovakia and Yugoslavia, England, Sweden, Poland, and many others.

Nevertheless, France was indeed a huge market for enameled ware, and many countries produced for France and the French taste. Europe was exporting a lot, especially after World War I; we even found traces of exports to the United States in the archives of the Saint Servais factory in Belgium.

European enameled ware has its own style, so specific that you can recognize it at a glance, even without being familiar with enameled ware. What makes it so special and attractive is the use of colors and wonderful designs, so close to nature or so abstract (depending on the period), but always striving for esthetic and artistic perfection.

Every piece, for those who can see it, has a fascinating little detail. It can be the shape or the decoration, the color of a flower, a butterfly, a bird trying to catch a bee, a landscape in winter, a sunrise, or simply the elegant curve of a handle or spout that makes it so unique. This unlimited variety of style and design makes French enameled ware so incredibly alive and charming that even people who have not seen it before have to stop and admire it.

Very rare coffee pot, rare in terms of the colors, flowers and shape, probably from Belgium, riveted, raised enamel. *Courtesy of The French Corner.* $595-660.

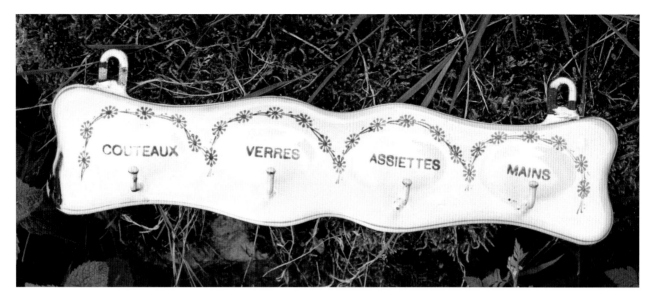

Kitchen towel-holder, Copenhagen or saxe design. *Courtesy of The French Corner.* $240-280

Soap and towel-holder with saxe or Copenhagen floral design often from Belgium. *Courtesy of The French Corner.* $250-280.

Match box, red with white raised French lettering, marbled green and white inside, riveted, from "SAINT SERVAIS" in Belgium, 7" tall. *Courtesy of The French Corner.* $240-260.

Beautiful coffee biggin, exceptional condition and design, 14" tall. *Courtesy of The French Corner.* $480-580.

Pink irrigator decorated with raised flowers. *Courtesy of The French Corner.* $220-250.

Hanger with roses and pansies, green shading effect. *Courtesy of The French Corner.* $240-260.

Coffee pot, uncommon red shading with floral design, 8" tall. *Courtesy of The French Corner.* $250-295.

Brown shading with raised pink roses is used on this beautiful coffee biggin, riveted, 14" tall. *Courtesy of The French Corner.* $480-560.

Teapot with white and blue shading effect and hand painted floral design, riveted piece. *Courtesy of The French Corner.* $280-350.

Matching "B&B" salt box. *Courtesy of The French Corner.* $350-380.

Floral design and red stripes are used on this hanger, typical of the "B&B" factory, Austria. *Courtesy of The French Corner.* $250-280.

Unusual canister set, black with plum design. *Courtesy of The French Corner.* $750-780.

Coffee biggin, partly hand painted floral design, red trim, 12" tall. *Courtesy of The French Corner.* $395-450.

Very rare small coffee pot, 6" tall, dark blue with raised floral design, flat handle, fastened spout, riveted knob, c. 1880. *Courtesy of The French Corner.* $320-390.

Coffee pot, riveted and raised floral design, 8" tall. *Courtesy of The French Corner.* $495-575.

Nice green shading with roses for this coffee biggin. *Courtesy of The French Corner.* $460-550.

White and red check pattern coffee pot, red trim and filter, 10" tall. *Courtesy of The French Corner.* $295-350.

Coffee pot with Art Nouveau floral design, riveted. *Courtesy of The French Corner.* $295-350.

Little coffee canister, rare size and design, decorated with flowers and butterfly, 5" tall. *Courtesy of The French Corner.* $130-180.

Hand painted pitcher, riveted and flat handle, c. 1860. *Courtesy of The French Corner.* $295-350.

Coffee pot with rare shape of handle and knob called bamboo style, decorated with flowers, and with its original chain on the lid. *Courtesy of The French Corner.* $350-450.

Nice kettle, hand painted and riveted, 10" tall. Landscape design with a lake and birds. *Courtesy of The French Corner.* $480-540.

Body pitcher with floral design, 16" tall. *Courtesy of The French Corner.* $395-450.

Very elegant coffee pot with filter, blue with white raised check design, 10" tall. *Courtesy of The French Corner.* $295-350.

Matching salt box. *Courtesy of The French Corner.* $250-280.

Spice canister set, six pieces, nice design. *Courtesy of The French Corner.* $550-650.

Charming and unusual little onion holder, 8" tall with fruit design. *Courtesy of The French Corner.* $350-395.

Beautiful blue and white mottled bucket with lid, 14" tall. *Courtesy of The French Corner.* $280-350.

Pitcher with raised floral design, riveted, 6" tall. *Courtesy of The French Corner.* $250-295.

Chicken wire kitchen utensil rack and coffee pot. *Courtesy of The French Corner.* Hanger $350-450, coffee pot $280-350.

Pink swirl bucket, 16" tall. *Courtesy of The French Corner.* $280-320.

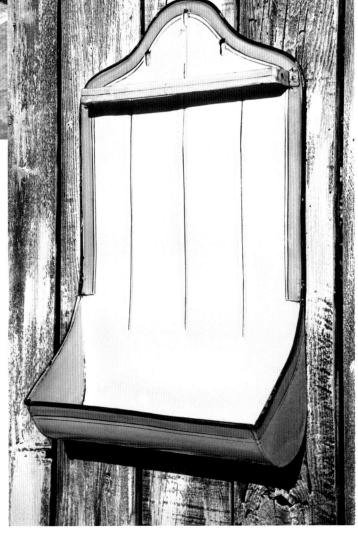

Rare kitchen utensil rack, hand decorated with gold and pink stripes, riveted. *Courtesy of The French Corner.* $240-260.

Charming little pitcher, raised floral design and lovely coloring. *Courtesy of The French Corner.* $295-340.

Rare green coffee pot with filter, rare raised floral design, 10" tall. *Courtesy of The French Corner.* $495-575.

Nice combination of colors on this complete coffee pot with an unusual yellow check design, 8" tall. *Courtesy of The French Corner.* $350-380.

Very charming coffee pot, green shading effect and floral and bird design, gives the impression of a window open on a landscape. Often this type of décor originated from east of France. *Courtesy of The French Corner.* $295-350.

Complete coffee pot, red background with white check design, probably from Belgium, 10" tall. *Courtesy of The French Corner.* $350-395.

Red and orange coffee pots with the same raised design, making us think of Christmas, 8" tall. It is interesting to compare two pieces with the same hand painted design. *Courtesy of The French Corner.* $295-250 each.

Wonderful coffee pot, unusual turquoise background, bird, flowers and butterfly design. *Courtesy of The French Corner.* $750-850.

Back of the coffee pot at left, with floral design only.

Coffee biggin with original lid and filter, white with hand painted floral and bird design, 14" tall. *Courtesy of The French Corner.* $650-750.

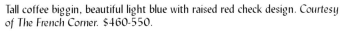
Tall coffee biggin, beautiful light blue with raised red check design. *Courtesy of The French Corner.* $460-550.

Kitchen utensil rack, blue shading with pansy flowers. *Courtesy of The French Corner.* $250-280.

Sweet little coffee pot, butterflies and flowers. *Courtesy of The French Corner.* $295-320.

Canister set decorated in raised enamel with French gothic lettering. *Courtesy of The French Corner.* $680-720.

Rare shape for this water pitcher, 14" tall, *Courtesy of The French Corner.* $250-280.

Milk container matching the canister set above. *Courtesy of The French Corner.* $320-350.

Child's set, fifteen pieces, riveted, 1" to 2" tall. *Courtesy of The French Corner.* $950-1,150.

Coffee biggin, hand painted floral design, 12" tall.
Courtesy of The French Corner. $320-360.

Beautiful body pitcher, hand painted birds and flowers, riveted.
Courtesy of The French Corner. $640-750.

Coffee pot with lace and floral design, hand painted, unusual
and rare design. *Courtesy of The French Corner.* $350-450.

Coffee set with pink shading and pansy flowers from "JAPY," France. Very rare set. *Courtesy of The French Corner.* $750-850.

Salt box with beautiful landscape, early piece. *Courtesy of The French Corner.* $290-350

Coffee pot with white and blue shading, rose and pansy design, origin "JAPY," France, 9" tall. *Courtesy of The French Corner* $350-395.

Coffee pot, green with brown trim, 10" tall. *Courtesy of The French Corner.* $180-220.

Coffee pot with filter, riveted piece with raised enamel floral design, 8" tall. *Courtesy of The French Corner.* $550-595.

Collection of body pitchers, variety of colors, designs, and periods. *Courtesy of The French Corner.* $250-350 each.

Kettle, yellow with green trim, 10" tall. *Courtesy of The French Corner.* $250-295.

Hand painted coffee pot, 8" tall. Fastened spout, riveted, beautiful floral design. *Courtesy of The French Corner.* $250-295.

Nice little coffee pot with filter, green and white coloring, Émailleries du Loiret, France, 9" tall. *Courtesy of The French Corner.* $350-395.

Wall utensil holder, floral design, c. 1885, 14" tall. *Courtesy of The French Corner.* $360-395.

Soup tureen with blue shading and floral design. *Courtesy of The French Corner.* $320-380.

Coffee pot with filter, fastened spout and riveted, beautiful raised floral design, 10" tall. *Courtesy of The French Corner.* $680-700.

Beautiful coffee pot, rare shape, copy of ceramic, hand painted and riveted. *Courtesy of The French Corner.* $295-360.

Chapter Two

Styles and Designs

Strange as it may seem, there are less terms used to describe non-figurative designs in Europe than in the United States. The words *marbré* for marble, *veiné* for swirl, or *émail granité* for granito are currently used, but that about sums it up. In order to use a common language, we will be using expressions like "chicken wire," "droopy check," and others explained later on, which are commonly understood in the United States.

Many non-figurative designs exist, created by the projection of enamel on the piece or by different thicknesses of the enamel. The most

Kitchen utensil rack, blue and white marbled, 18" tall. *Courtesy of The French Corner.* $180-220.

Coffee pots, blue and white mottled, one with filter and one without, 8" and 10" tall. *Courtesy of The French Corner.* With filter $250-280, without filter $220-250.

common effect is marbled, obtained by using two layers (coats) of enamel of different colors, the second coat always white and thin. You will find many colors of marbled; blue is the easiest to find while the greens and red are the most popular.

Another term commonly used is "mottled" or "snow on the mountain." This refers to a design that is close to the marbled effect, however the second layer of enamel is thicker and less precise: when you touch the piece you feel a granulated effect that the marbled does not have. This design exists in many colors.

The swirl, also based on the combination of two colors, gives the effect of "trickling water" along the piece in equal proportions. This design can also be found on many American enameled pieces, which makes it more familiar to the American public, especially when it is in gray or blue. Swirl can be found in numerous colors, such as red, light to dark blue, and many shades of green. And let's not forget pink, which is always wonderful and refreshing on European pieces.

"End of the day" coffee pot, pink and green coloring. *Courtesy of The French Corner.* $350-395.

Body pitcher with swirl design, 15" tall. *Courtesy of The French Corner.* $280-320.

When the design includes a combination of at least three colors, the term "end of the day" is used. More than three colors can be used, even four or six on the same piece. These are often early pieces, and are rare due to their age. They are extremely sought after by collectors for the fascinating effects sometimes produced by the unexpected combination of colors. The mélange of green with white and pink is a very popular "end of the day" combination; you can also find blue with pink and white, brown with pink and green, some grays, and also black with red and yellow. Many other unexpected combinations exist as well.

Another very popular design is called the "chicken wire" pattern; it is based on the combination of two colors. The white layer gives an octagonal effect all over the piece like chicken wire, hence the name. Chicken wire on older pieces is often thicker and smaller with light blue as a background; on later pieces the blue is darker with the chicken wire effect being thinner and larger. This design was, and still is, very popular in northern Europe, especially in Germany. Most of the backgrounds were blue, but other colors like red and green were also used – these are very rare and of course highly sought after.

Chicken wire salt box, blue French lettering, *Courtesy of The French Corner.* $380-420.

The design called "droopy check" is close to "chicken wire" but gives the effect of a checkerboard falling apart — or of a water drop streaming along the piece. It is very popular in France and can be found in several colors. The most collected color is red, followed by a tender pink, light blue or orange, and sometimes, but rarely, green. This design is highly collectible today.

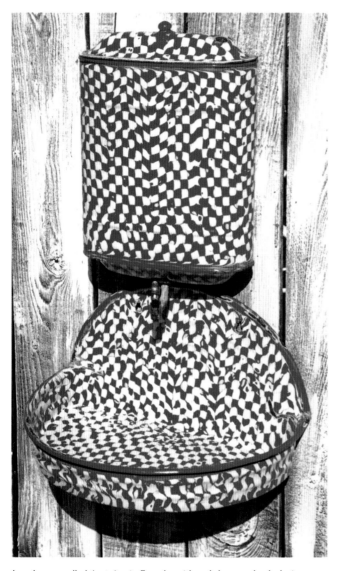

Lavabo set called *fontaine* in French, with red droopy check design, very rare and complete, in excellent condition. *Courtesy of The French Corner.* $950-1,200.

Non-figurative or plain color designs are not specific to a certain period of time, but were produced from the late nineteenth century to the end of the 1950s. These designs cannot be classified as easily as the figurative pieces, which are more often representative of a certain period of time based on their style. So for age determination, we must also take into consideration the techniques used to build the pieces.

The very first figurative pieces were built and decorated completely by hand, just as would have been done for a piece in faience or porcelain. We even have names of painters that were found in some of the factory archives. These qualified workers used little enameled plates, passed on from generation to generation, with a certain design that they employed as a guideline. The motif was always inspired by nature — flowers, birds, insects, or landscapes were often used.

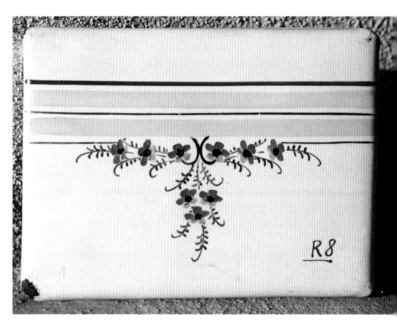

Enamel plate with number on it, probably a worker's design sample, 4" tall. *Courtesy of The French Corner.* $180-195.

On the oldest pieces, the motif was always very thick; it is called "raised enamel" and was added onto single color backgrounds that were often blue. Other colors were also used, such as pink, green, red, brown, and the most rare, black. There are also hand painted pieces that were not done in "raised enamel" — this does not mean that they are less old than the raised enamel ones, or less valuable.

Starting around the beginning of the 1920s, more stylized designs — like the checkered or geometrical patterns — were more commonly used.

Complete red spice set with raised white stripes and gothic lettering, rare quality. Includes canisters for pepper, tea, tapioca, chicory, coffee and the tallest for sugar. *Courtesy of The French Corner.* $650-750.

Matching salt box with original wooden lid. *Courtesy of The French Corner.* $295-350.

Chicken wire coffee biggin, red trim, riveted piece, 12" tall. *Courtesy of The French Corner.* $350-380.

Body pitcher with airbrushed design, 15" tall. *Courtesy of The French Corner.* $350-450.

Tall coffee biggin with hand painted decor. *Courtesy of The French Corner.* $340-380.

Teapot, pitcher, and canister, red shading effect with hand painted flowers, riveted pieces. *Courtesy of The French Corner.* Tea pot $280-350, pitcher $260-280, canister $140-160.

A bird, butterfly, and flowers decorate this hand painted and rare irrigator, riveted, 12" tall. *Courtesy of The French Corner.* $350-380.

Very charming coffee pot with hand painted flowers, 10" tall. *Courtesy of The French Corner.* $495-560.

Small vegetable bucket, Copenhagen flowers, riveted, 12" tall. *Courtesy of The French Corner.* $280-320.

Spice set, yellow and green trim, French lettering, signed "Sphinx." *Courtesy of The French Corner.* $550-580.

Very rare footed teapot, fastened spout, riveted, original wooden handle, hand painted with two different designs, c. 1850-1885. *Courtesy of Adría Iwanyk & John Popko, Private Collection.* $750-850.

The other side of this wonderful teapot is decorated with pansies. *Courtesy of Adría Iwanyk & John Popko, Private Collection.*

Pink kettle, riveted piece, 12" tall. *Courtesy of The French Corner.* $250-280.

Lovely floral design on a white hanger. *Courtesy of The French Corner.* $240-260.

Coffee canister set, white with red polka dots. *Courtesy of The French Corner,* $350-420.

Hanger with fruit design. *Courtesy of The French Corner.* $240-260.

Kitchen utensil rack, blue and white shading with floral design. *Courtesy of The French Corner.* $240-260.

Very rare kitchen utensil rack with hand painted flowers, perfect condition and rare design. *Courtesy of The French Corner.* $380-450.

Red and white mottled bucket and body pitcher. *Courtesy of The French Corner.* $550-650 for set.

"JAPY" salt box, decorated with rose and pansy design, white and pink shading effect, original wooden lid, 10" tall. *Courtesy of The French Corner.* $295-375.

Detail of the floral design. *Courtesy of The French Corner.*

Coffee pot with roses, probably German. *Courtesy of The French Corner.* $280-295.

Lovely coffee pot with garlands of roses, probably German. *Courtesy of The French Corner.* $295-340.

Unusual floral design on this pitcher. *Courtesy of The French Corner.* $295-350.

Lovely coffee pot with unusual design. *Courtesy of The French Corner.* $295-320.

"End of the day" set of pans, rare coloring of red, blue, and white. *Courtesy of The French Corner.* $750-850.

Bread tray, blue shading and raised floral design. *Courtesy of The French Corner.* $380-420.

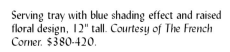

Serving tray with blue shading effect and raised floral design, 12" tall. *Courtesy of The French Corner.* $380-420.

Lovely pitcher with hand painted raised floral design,
6" tall. *Courtesy of The French Corner.* $250-295.

Coffee biggin with hand painted raised floral design, 12" tall. *Courtesy of
The French Corner.* $295-350.

Exceptional coffee pot, pink with very sophisticated and thick enamel floral design. *Courtesy of The French Corner.* $620-700.

Coffee biggin, "Émailleries du Loiret," French, blue and white coloring, 15" tall. *Courtesy of The French Corner.* $385-420.

Small coffee biggin with rare floral design on pink shading. *Courtesy of The French Corner.* $350-395.

Blue and white check design coffee pot with original filter, 10" tall. *Courtesy of The French Corner.* $250-285.

Salt box, red and white check design. *Courtesy of The French Corner.* $250-280.

Two red and white coffee pots, mottled or "snow on the mountain" design on left, marbled design on right. *Courtesy of The French Corner.* $250-270 each.

Very sophisticated "end of the day" design on this irrigator, riveted. *Courtesy of The French Corner.* $220-260.

Coffee pot with green shading, hand painted, decorated with a beautiful winter landscape. *Courtesy of The French Corner.* $495-580.

Coffee pot or beer pitcher with very rare spout shape, also rare hand painted floral design. *Courtesy of The French Corner.* $550-620.

Teapot with raised floral design on brown background, riveted piece, 6" tall. *Courtesy of The French Corner.* $450-520.

Charming complete spice set with French lettering, "B&B," Austria.
Courtesy of The French Corner. $580-660.

Blue marbled coffee pot, 12" tall. *Courtesy of The French Corner.* $250-295.

Coffee pot, raised vine leaves design, original filter, riveted, 10" tall. *Courtesy of The French Corner.* $495-550.

Rare coffee biggin, very rare blue shading with floral design. *Courtesy of The French Corner.* $580-620.

Coffee pot with beautiful bird and flowers design, raised enamel. *Courtesy of The French Corner.* $660-680.

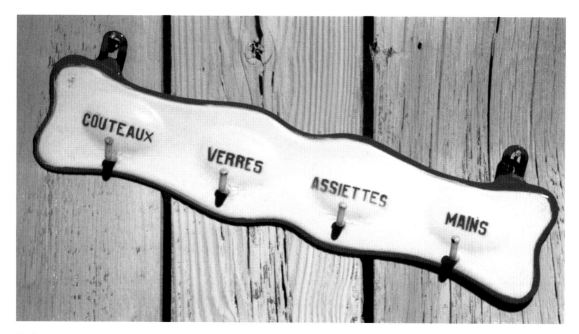

Kitchen towel holder, white and red trim, French words *couteaux* for knives, *verre* for glasses, *assiettes* for plates, *mains* for hands. *Courtesy of The French Corner.* $240-260.

Interesting coffee pot with blue check on red background, lined with yellow, 8" tall. *Courtesy of The French Corner.* $220-250.

Blue soap holder with gold decoration, 4" tall. *Courtesy of The French Corner.* $95-110.

Body pitcher with pink and green shading effect, hand painted. *Courtesy of The French Corner.* $490-580.

Art Deco coffee biggin, nice color combination. *Courtesy of The French Corner.* $360-380.

Pitcher with floral design, 8" tall. *Courtesy of The French Corner.* $150-195.

Art deco salt box, orange and blue check design, red lettering. *Courtesy of The French Corner.* $240-260.

Body pitcher with very elegant raised enamel design, riveted. *Courtesy of The French Corner.* $580-620.

Lovely hand painted pitcher, 8" tall. *Courtesy of The French Corner.* $250-280.

Chapter Three

History of Enameled Ware

Enameling techniques were known in many ancient civilizations, such as Egypt and Mesopotamia, where they were essentially used for jewelry. During the eighteenth century, the first tentative use of enameling for kitchenware was made. However, the enamel layer was not resistant enough to high temperature variations, so it cracked easily and was dangerous for cooking and eating purposes.

It was not until the mid-nineteenth century that enough progress was made in manufacturing techniques for enamel to be commonly used in kitchenware. Enamel soon became very popular, as it was inexpensive, much easier to clean than copper or other metals, and had a modern look. In addition, the ceramic-inspired shapes and the attractive decoration gave enameled ware a tremendous boost. Flowers and landscapes were very popular and were always hand painted from the mid-nineteenth century up to the early 1920s, after which decal or spray techniques were more commonly used.

From the late nineteenth century to 1910, enameled ware was influenced by the "Art Nouveau" style, featuring wonderful vegetal designs and more curly lines. These pieces are extremely rare due to the limited period of production when Art Nouveau was popular. Afterwards, the "Art Deco" style took over, bringing with it many geometric designs. Enameled ware slowly departed from an imitation of porcelain design to find its own independence and style. The general shape of items changed, with more square and geometrical lines (especially for handles) used. Octagonal canisters and checkered designs were preferred and commonly used. Even flowers were more stylized to correspond more with the tastes of the time.

Enameled ware enjoyed its last period of success from c. 1940 to 1960, when decal designs were nearly the only ones used. Nevertheless, enameled ware became less and less popular after around 1950. The use of aluminum had begun in the early 1930s, and the appearance of plastic for certain kitchenware items (which was considered more modern at the time and was less expensive), also accelerated the demise of enameled ware.

In addition, World War II led to many changes in the European way of life. The appearance of electrical appliances and bathrooms in every home made certain items – lavabo sets and body pitchers, for example – too archaic and nonfunctional. Slowly, certain items that did not correspond to the current way of living were no longer produced and were replaced by others. Enameled ware lost more and more of its esthetic nature, becoming only simple and functional. The majority of factories closed at that time or changed their production to suit the need of the times.

Today, some countries are still producing enameled ware; they include Poland (where pieces are signed "Made in Poland"), some other eastern European countries, Portugal, and even France. These pieces are not meant to be copies, as they have a new design that corresponds to today's tastes and are often plain color pieces. For the moment there are no copies of French enameled ware, other than perhaps some pieces coming from China that are signed "Made in China." Confusing those with the originals is impossible, however, given the differences in quality and style. The esthetic nature of old pieces with respect to design and technique is far superior to what is made today and the two cannot be compared in any way.

Very rare three piece child's set, includes lavabo set, body pitcher, basin and bucket, hand painted and riveted, bamboo handle, 5" to 6" tall. *Courtesy of The French Corner.* $950-1,050.

Another view of the body pitcher from the wonderful set on the opposite page. It is 6" tall with a lovely floral design. *Courtesy of The French Corner.*

Bread basket, partly hand painted, floral design. *Courtesy of The French Corner.* $160-180.

Match box and salt box with large red and white check design, one red and white and the other the opposite, highly collectible model. *Courtesy of The French Corner.* Match box $240-260, salt box $300-350.

Large white and red check design coffee pot with filter and spice canister set. *Courtesy of The French Corner.* Coffee pot $480-550, canister set $450-550.

Exceptional pitcher, 6" tall, with raised, hand painted floral design and ribbon with French lettering *sois sincère* ("be sincere"), extremely rare, c. 1850-1875. *Courtesy of Adria Iwanyk & John Popko, Private Collection.* $550-560.

Another view of this wonderful pitcher, showing the flat handle. *Courtesy of Adria Iwanyk & John Popko, Private Collection.*

Egg holders with gold design, c. 1885. *Courtesy of The French Corner.* $95 each.

Lovely and rare shape for this little coffee pot, floral design and riveted, 8" tall. *Courtesy of The French Corner.* $380-420.

Nice white and red check design on this kitchen utensil rack. *Courtesy of The French Corner.* $220-240.

Body pitcher and bucket, white with raised red lines. *Courtesy of The French Corner.* $550-620 for set.

Beautiful coffee biggin, blue and white shading with hand painted landscape, 12" tall. *Courtesy of The French Corner.* $380-450.

Blue and white shading coffee pot with filter, Émailleries du Loiret. *Courtesy of The French Corner.* $290-350.

Utensil rack with Copenhagen floral design. *Courtesy of The French Corner.* $180-200.

Coffee pot with rare shape, bamboo style handle and knob with Copenhagen flowers, beautiful piece. *Courtesy of The French Corner.* $450-520.

Unusual jar with handles and lid, 10" tall. *Courtesy of The French Corner.* $260-280.

Lovely and complete coffee pot with light pink background, unusual floral design and colors. *Courtesy of The French Corner.* $595-680.

Matching pitcher shows more detail of this charming décor. *Courtesy of The French Corner.* $560-595.

Coffee biggin with rare yellow shading and flowers, probably "JAPY," France. *Courtesy of The French Corner.* $480-550.

Coffee biggin, pink shading and floral design. *Courtesy of The French Corner.* $420-495.

Coffee biggin, pansy floral design with white and blue shading, 15 " tall. *Courtesy of The French Corner.* $450-550.

Wonderful coffee pot with red and white plum design, gold décor still visible, original filter, 10" tall. *Courtesy of The French Corner.* $350-450.

Dark brown coffee pot with flat handle, riveted and raised floral design, rare piece, c. 1850-1885. *Courtesy of The French Corner* $550-650.

Set of five pans with plum design. *Courtesy of The French Corner.* $550 for set.

Exceptional complete canister set with hand painted flowers, signed "Etoile" Belgium. *Courtesy of The French Corner.* $1,600-1,800.

Detail of the very sophisticated canister set above. *Courtesy of The French Corner.*

Tall coffee biggin with hand painted flowers and bird. *Courtesy of The French Corner.* $750-800.

Wonderful little coffee pot, lovely raised floral design,
8" tall. *Courtesy of The French Corner.* $580-650.

Blue coffee pot with white check design, 10" tall. *Courtesy of The French
Corner.* $220-250.

Wonderful coffee biggin, red and white raised check design, 10" tall.
Courtesy of The French Corner. $380-450.

Elegant teapot with blue stripes and garlands of flowers, origin "B&B."
Courtesy of The French Corner. $280-320.

Unusual green color on this coffee pot, probably from Germany. *Courtesy of The French Corner.* $350-380.

Pitcher with very rare black background in raised enamel, decorated with two birds and flowers, riveted, flat handle, c. 1850. *Courtesy of The French Corner.* $585-650.

Lovely coffee pot, partly hand painted, German origin, 8" tall. *Courtesy of The French Corner.* $260-295.

Large blue and white shading teapot, riveted, 8" tall. *Courtesy of The French Corner.* $250-295.

Unusual shape for this coffee pot, riveted and raised enamel design, flat handle, 8" tall. *Courtesy of The French Corner.* $420-480.

Sweet pastel coloring on this small coffee pot, raised enamel. *Courtesy of The French Corner.* $340-360.

Rare shape for this 13" tall kettle with raised floral design. The shape is called "Louis Philippe" in reference to the style of this period in France. *Courtesy of The French Corner.* $750-820.

Unusual shading color is used on this tall, rose decorated coffee biggin. *Courtesy of The French Corner.* $580-620.

Beautiful body pitcher with hand painted floral design, 12" tall. *Courtesy of The French Corner.* $450-550.

Coffee pot, charming green with raised floral design, 6" tall; white coffee pot,
"B&B" Austria, 8" tall. *Courtesy of The French Corner.* $295-350 each.

Red and white swirl canister set and coffee pot, French lettering. *Courtesy
of The French Corner.* Canister set $600-650, coffee pot $250-275.

Spice canister set, probably part of a twelve piece set, with Copenhagen flowers. *Courtesy of The French Corner.* $550-650.

Coffee pot with nice combination of colors, partly hand painted. *Courtesy of The French Corner.* $260-295.

Butter dish with raised enamel floral design, very elegant piece in excellent condition, 4" tall. *Courtesy of The French Corner.* $320-380.

Coffee pot with filter, red and white check design, 10" tall. *Courtesy of The French Corner.* $295-350.

Coffee biggin, unusual color in raised enamel, riveted and fastened spout, 15" tall. *Courtesy of The French Corner.* $555-595.

Very rare and exceptional creamer, hand painted and riveted, design and shape typical of pieces c. 1850, 4" tall. *Courtesy of The French Corner.* $550-650.

Small pitcher with red and orange shading, 6" tall. *Courtesy of The French Corner.* $65-85.

Raised enamel coffee pot, floral design with butterfly, 10" tall, "Etoile" Belgium. *Courtesy of The French Corner.* $495-575.

Yellow pitcher with green trim, 8" tall. *Courtesy of The French Corner.* $85-120.

Coffee pot, rare green with white check design, lined with black. *Courtesy of The French Corner.* $295-350.

Towel and soap holder in chicken wire design, 10" tall. *Courtesy of The French Corner.* $250-280.

Coffee biggin, white and red check design. *Courtesy of The French Corner.* $250-295.

Art Deco salt box, white and blue check design. *Courtesy of The French Corner.* $220-250.

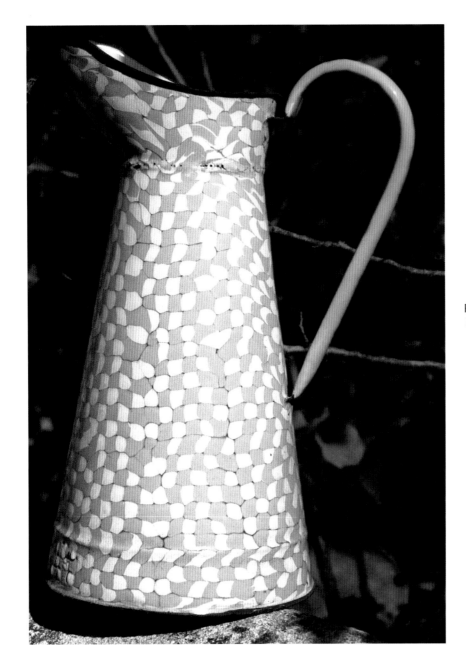

Rare body pitcher with light blue droopy check design, 15" tall. *Courtesy of The French Corner.* $980-1,100.

Wonderful and rare complete spice set with blue droopy check design and French lettering in red. *Courtesy of The French Corner.* $1,100-1,200.

Coffee pot, pink shading with roses, 8" tall.
Courtesy of The French Corner. $280-295.

Coffee pot with unusual floral design and composition, raised enamel.
Courtesy of The French Corner. $480-550.

Chapter Four

Determining Age

It is very difficult to precisely date a piece of enameled ware, although we can often determine at least the approximate time period in which they were made. Sometimes we can be more precise with later pieces if they appear in dated catalogues we have found. Nevertheless, it is helpful to take two factors into consideration when dating a piece: the first is the design and the second is the technique used to build the piece.

Technical characteristics are not always reliable, however, considering that some factories were using the old way of manufacturing for a longer period of time. This is why you will find pieces using the riveted technique on the main body that was obtained by machine. There is a paradox here, because if rivets are used then the bottom edges should be flat, yet we find some pieces with rounded edges (obtained by press) still with riveted parts instead of welded parts.

It is commonly accepted that the very first pieces date from the mid-nineteenth century. These pieces are easy to detect due to their rustic look: the entire body is made with different pieces of metal riveted together, the handles are flat and riveted, and the spout is fastened with two pieces of metal riveted to the main part. The knob will also be attached to the lid with a rivet. On coffee pots, the lid itself is attached to the pot; later, removable lids with filters became more popular. The more you can see the structure of the piece, the more you can be sure that it is old.

Another detail that can help identify older pieces is found in the decoration – often the lines of the structure and the rivets were painted with a color (usually brown) that was different from the main design. In addition, the weight of the piece can be a good indication of age; the older the piece the heavier it will be. This is due to the thickness of the enameled layer.

On older pieces you will notice the presence of a mark, often in gold lettering, that was applied to the bottom – though not systematically. These marks often represent a letter and numbers that we believe correspond to the serial number and the model reference. Some people believe that the letter may correspond to the initials of the worker's name. On younger pieces, these marks will be replaced by the name of the factory and also the country of production – unless a simple paper label has been applied to the piece, a label that often disappears.

With the advent of industrial progress, enameled ware pieces were made more and more by machine and only out of one piece of metal. The shape of the main body was obtained by press and the different parts were welded together. The knob of the lid was also pressed by machine out of one piece of metal, and the handles were round and welded. This technique dates approximately to the early 1920s. From 1930 up to the last period of production, only the styles and designs can be taken into account when determining the age of the piece.

While these criteria may be confusing or difficult, keep in mind that the most important thing about a piece is the feeling that it impresses on us. Dating information is nonetheless helpful and can be used to find your own way as a collector in this huge world that represents collectible enameled ware.

Brown coffee pot with fastened spout and flat handle, riveted, very thick raised floral design, c. 1850-1885, very rare piece probably from Belgium. *Courtesy of The French Corner.* $550-560.

Exceptional piece, extremely rare and in wonderful condition, this sugar container has a beautiful decor. *Courtesy of The French Corner.* $560-620.

Matching pitcher, same décor and condition, rare design. *Courtesy of The French Corner.* $560-620.

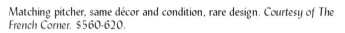

Beautiful body pitcher with rose and pansy design, probably of "JAPY," origin. *Courtesy of The French Corner.* $440-520.

Beautiful teapot with very sophisticated raised floral design. *Courtesy of The French Corner.* $595-650.

Exceptional hand painted pitcher, beautiful floral design, 6" tall. *Courtesy of The French Corner.* $450-550.

Detail of lettering and flowers on the canister set below. *Courtesy of The French Corner.*

Very rare and exceptional coffee canister set, mint condition, decorated with pansies, probably "JAPY" in origin. *Courtesy of The French Corner.* $750-800.

Two complete coffee pots, with filters and beautiful pure colors, "SAINT-SERVAIS," Belgium. *Courtesy of The French Corner.* $230-250 each.

Art Deco body pitcher in raised enamel lined with gold. *Courtesy of The French Corner.* $480-550.

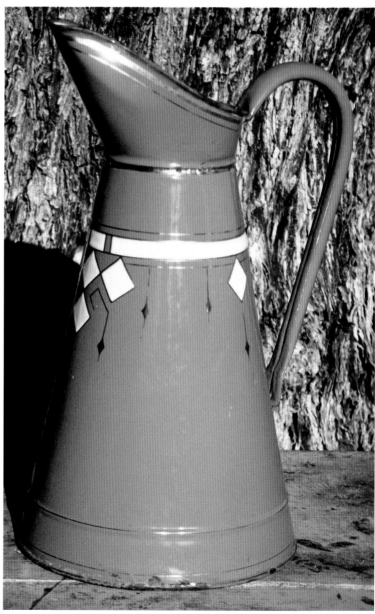

Rare enamel plate with oriental floral design, raised enamel, 16" tall, exceptional piece. *Courtesy of The French Corner.* $750-850.

Complete canister set with garland of roses and green trim, French lettering, origin "B&B," Austria. *Courtesy of The French Corner.* $680-795.

Detail of the bird, a very sophisticated and elegant painting. *Courtesy of The French Corner.*

Exceptional coffee biggin with brown shading effect, hand painted raised enamel design of bird, flowers, and butterfly. The brown background contrasts beautifully with the colors of the flowers and the bird. *Courtesy of The French Corner.* $750-820.

Other side of the coffee biggin, flowers and butterfly, riveted piece, fastened spout, c. 1885-1900. *Courtesy of The French Corner.*

Complete six piece spice canister set, red with raised white and black check design, French lettering. Canisters from largest to smallest: sugar, coffee, flour, pasta, tea, spice. Signed "DUCO," origin Czechoslovakia. *Courtesy of The French Corner.* $650-750.

Beautiful bucket with lid and wooden handle, riveted, hand painted floral design, c. 1885. *Courtesy of The French Corner.* $750-850.

Kitchen utensil rack, blue trim, chicken wire design, riveted piece. The bottom is fastened on the sides. *Courtesy of The French Corner.* $250-295.

Coffee pot in mint condition, rare background, rare floral design. Courtesy of The French Corner. $680-695.

Green swirl coffee biggin with blue trim, 12" tall. Courtesy of The French Corner. $295-350.

Very rare coffee pot, rare for its colors and floral design, typical of the 1800s. Courtesy of The French Corner. $580-620.

Milk boiler with original lid, garland of roses, "B&B," Austria, 6" tall. *Courtesy of The French Corner.* $200-280.

Pitcher with "end of the day" design, pink, green and white coloring, riveted piece, 9" tall. *Courtesy of The French Corner.* $395-420.

Hand painted teapot with band of pink and floral design, 5" tall. *Courtesy of The French Corner.* $250-295.

Teapot with pink shading and flowers, probably from Austria. *Courtesy of The French Corner.* $295-350.

Beautiful raised enamel coffee pot, decorated with roses. *Courtesy of The French Corner.* $580-650.

"End of the day" body pitcher, riveted piece. *Courtesy of The French Corner.* $650-680.

Two tureens, c. 1880, with hand painted floral design, riveted, rare articles typical of this era. *Courtesy of The French Corner.* $420-480 each.

Coffee pot with very sophisticated raised floral design, riveted and fastened spout. *Courtesy of The French Corner.* $580-650.

Tall coffee biggin with green and white shading, floral design. *Courtesy of The French Corner.* $420-520.

Green shading with roses is the design for this pitcher. *Courtesy of The French Corner,* $295-350.

Pink pitcher with butterfly and pansy flowers design, raised enamel, riveted. *Courtesy of The French Corner.* $395-480.

Pitcher with raised enamel floral design, riveted piece, 8" tall. *Courtesy of The French Corner.* $275-295.

Water pitcher with flowers, pink trim. *Courtesy of The French Corner.* $280-320.

Small tray with raised floral design typical of the 1800s. *Courtesy of The French Corner.* $320-370.

Nice brown shading on this coffee pot with roses. *Courtesy of The French Corner,* $550-620.

Pitcher with floral design and pink shading effect. *Courtesy of The French Corner.* $220-250.

Blue coffee pot with raised floral design, 8" tall. *Courtesy of The French Corner.* $495-595.

Coffee pot with very elegant and sophisticated raised floral design, original lid and filter, riveted piece, 9" tall. *Courtesy of The French Corner.* $650-680.

Coffee pot, white and green shading with floral design, 10" tall. *Courtesy of The French Corner.* $350-395.

Wonderful water pitcher, blue and pink shading with hand painted flowers, 6" tall. *Courtesy of The French Corner.* $380-395.

Water pitcher and bucket, riveted pieces and fastened, ivory color with gold decoration. *Courtesy of The French Corner.* $550-650 for set.

Exceptional salt box, hand painted with green shading effect. *Courtesy of The French Corner.* $480-560.

Another view of this beautiful salt box. *Courtesy of The French Corner.*

Large coffee biggin with hand painted blue flowers, riveted. *Courtesy of The French Corner.* $350-450.

Wonderful canister set, completely hand painted with floral design, probably part of a twelve piece canister set. *Courtesy of The French Corner.* $800-880.

Detail of those lovely hand painted flowers on the sugar canister above. *Courtesy of The French Corner.*

Pretty pink coffee pot with pansies, 8" tall. *Courtesy of The French Corner.* $250-295.

Very exceptional and rare body pitcher, rare raised enamel floral design, rare handle (bamboo style), riveted. *Courtesy of The French Corner.* $950-1,000.

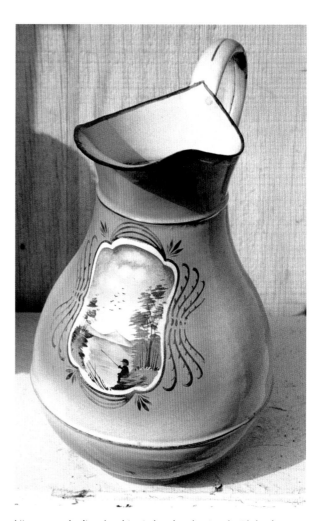

Nice green shading for this pitcher, hand painted with landscape. *Courtesy of The French Corner.* $495-560.

Wonderful variety of flowers on this coffee pot in raised enamel. *Courtesy of The French Corner.* $595-680.

Child's set "end of the day" design teapot, riveted, 4" tall. *Courtesy of The French Corner.* $350-480.

Pitcher with white and blue shading effect, rose and pansy design, 8" tall. *Courtesy of The French Corner.* $295-350.

Coffee pot with raised floral design, 8" tall. *Courtesy of The French Corner.* $280-340.

Teapot with white and red trim, decorated with red line, "SAINT-SERVAIS," Belgium, 6" tall. *Courtesy of The French Corner.* $220-250.

Hand painted body pitcher, pink shading and flowers. *Courtesy of The French Corner.* $480-550.

Detail of the handle on this very elegant piece. *Courtesy of The French Corner.*

Elegant coffee biggin, riveted, origin "B&B," Austria. *Courtesy of The French Corner.* $350-380.

Coffee pot with filter and original lid, red check design, lined with black, 10" tall. *Courtesy of The French Corner.* $295-350.

Charming little complete coffee pot with raised butterfly and flowers. *Courtesy of The French Corner.* $580-660.

Lovely coffee pot with hand painted flowers and butterfly. *Courtesy of The French Corner.* $380-420.

Lovely blue match box with raised lettering in French. *Courtesy of The French Corner.* $180-220.

Blue body pitcher, early piece, riveted, *Courtesy of The French Corner.* $220-250.

Chapter Five

What to Collect

Many items can be found in enameled ware, and all can be collected. The most famous of course are the coffee pots, but other choices, including match boxes, salt boxes, and canister sets, are also very popular.

You will find several kinds of coffee pots, which can be loosely put into two categories. The first category consists of coffee pots with removable lids and filters, which can be further subdivided into those that have removable filters without handles with the lid unattached, and those with a handle on the filter, called "coffee biggins." The second category consists of coffee pots with the lid attached to the body. Their sizes can vary significantly, from the smallest you can imagine to the largest.

Match boxes also vary in size, but what varies most are the strikers. Match boxes can have a striker or even sometimes two (one on the lid and one on the front) and are also found without a striker. They also come with or without writing on them (i.e., the word *allumettes*).

Salt boxes can have a wooden lid or an enameled lid, regardless of age period. Like match boxes, they can have writing on them (*sel*) or no writing.

Canister sets can be classified into three categories:

1. The coffee set. This set has only three canisters of the same size: coffee, sugar, and chicory.
2. The spice set. Traditionally a set of six, but sometimes found with more. The sizes are graduated and the canisters may have writing or not. You will usually find one for sugar (*sucre*), coffee (*café*), flour (*farine*), pasta (*pâtes*), tea (*thé*), and spices (*épices*). The names can vary from one set to another, depending on the individual needs.
3. The spice set of twelve canisters. Often made up of older pieces and rarely complete, these sets will have six large and six small canisters. They can also have writing on them or not.

The most collected design and the most difficult to find in the world of enamel ware, light blue stripes with garlands of roses, "B&B," Austria. This picture shows the wonderful design impact of displaying a complete kitchen set in a house. *Courtesy of The French Corner.* On the bottom shelf are a 12" tall pan $380-450, and a milk carrier $450-480.

These are the most collected items, but we have to remember that they often represent only pieces of a complete set, going from the kitchen to the bathroom. Complete sets are very rare. We can get an idea of what comprised a set from the different catalogues produced by shops like *La Samaritaine*, *Galerie La Fayette*, or *Bon Marché* in France, which had their own line of enameled ware at the time.

The kitchen utensil rack (hanger) is often a piece that surprises the American public. The rack (hanger) part was made to hang utensils on the wall, while the bottom part was used as a drip pan. These pieces can vary in size and have from two to six utensils.

Another item that is more common for European enameled ware is the milk boiler; this is a kind of pan that has a lid with holes in it to keep the milk from boiling over.

Many other pieces of enameled ware can be added to a collection: series of pans of every size with lids, towel holders, irrigators, pitchers for milk, water or beer, body pitchers, buckets, lavabo sets, chamber pots, trivets, laundry sets to hang on the wall, egg cups, salt and pepper sets, candle sticks, and soap dishes – the choice is huge. Sometimes unexpected pieces can be found, such as chimney mantels, picture frames, dish dryers, cups with lids, trays, lid holders, letter holders, umbrella stands, and samovars. Children's sets or salesmen's samples are very rare and highly collectible. The list is long and always incomplete, given that we still find a few unexpected pieces – especially from the nineteenth century – that were occasionally produced by special order or for special events.

Salt box. *Courtesy of The French Corner.* $480-550.

The mixture of the light pink, green, and blue gives a very fresh feeling to these pieces, and the stripes a very elegant look. This partly explains the success of this design. *Courtesy of The French Corner.*

Beautiful little match box. *Courtesy of The French Corner.* $560-620.

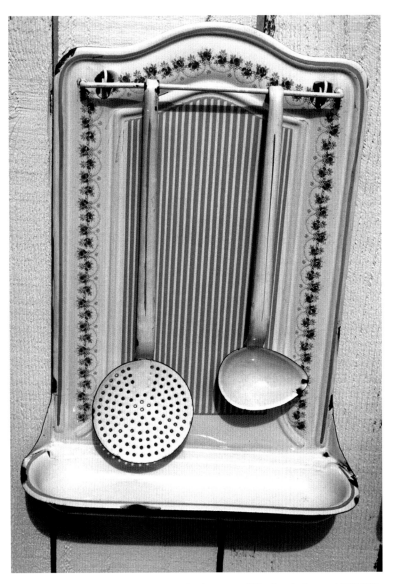

Kitchen utensil rack with utensils. *Courtesy of The French Corner.* $595-680.

Complete coffee pot with filter. *Courtesy of The French Corner.* $680-760.

One of the most popular canister sets, this one is complete.
Courtesy of The French Corner. $1,100-1,200.

Called a syrup pitcher in the USA but used to warm coffee in Europe, rare piece, 8" tall.
Courtesy of The French Corner. $395-450.

Laundry set, rare in this model. *Courtesy of The French Corner.* $580-650.

Two pitchers, 4" and 8" tall, rare in this model. *Courtesy of The French Corner,* $350-380 each.

Set of pans, five pieces. *Courtesy of The French Corner.* $180-220 each.

Beautiful teapot. *Courtesy of The French Corner.* $680-750.

Rare pitcher with raised enamel décor, bird, flowers, and fruits, c. 1880. Courtesy of The French Corner. $520-580.

Unusual cup with lid, raised floral design, 5 " tall, Courtesy of Adria Iwanyk & John Popko, Private Collection. $250-350.

Exceptional coffee pot, flat handle, riveted, fastened spout, hand painted floral design, c. 1850-1885, Belgium. Courtesy of The French Corner. $650-690.

Chicken wire body pitcher, riveted. *Courtesy of The French Corner.* $450-550.

Large coffee biggin, light blue with raised floral design, 14" tall. *Courtesy of The French Corner.* $350-380.

Two chicken wire pitchers, 10" tall blue and very rare 8" tall red. *Courtesy of The French Corner.* Blue $280-320, red $450-550.

Elegant coffee pot with filter, decorated with roses, 12" tall. *Courtesy of The French Corner.* $360-480.

Set of five pans in the same design as the coffee pot at left, marbled white and green inside. *Courtesy of The French Corner.* $550-650 for set.

Very famous large red and white check design on a 10" tall coffee pot with filter. *Courtesy of The French Corner.* $395-450.

Vegetable bucket, *Légumes* in French, beige with green trim and lettering, 14" tall. *Courtesy of The French Corner.* $350-380.

Exceptional coffee biggin, red background with raised floral design, 14" tall. *Courtesy of The French Corner.* $450-550.

Red with white polka dot set, DUCO, Czechoslovakia. *Courtesy of The French Corner.* $995-1,200 for set.

Exceptional *Amidon* canister, hand painted with riveted knob. *Courtesy of The French Corner.* $395-475.

Coffee biggin with floral design, "JAPY," France. *Courtesy of The French Corner.* $380-420.

Teapot with blue shading and roses. *Courtesy of The French Corner.* $295-320.

Serving tray with hand painted pansies, 13" tall. *Courtesy of The French Corner.* $480-550.

Charming design composition of roses, pansies, and butterfly on this raised enamel coffee pot. *Courtesy of The French Corner.* $595-650.

Small creamer, sophisticated raised floral design with butterfly. *Courtesy of The French Corner.* $295-350.

Coffee pot, wonderful green background with raised floral design and birds. *Courtesy of The French Corner.* $595-650.

Charming little coffee pot with floral design and filter, "B&B" Austria. *Courtesy of The French Corner.* $250-295.

The other side of the coffee pot has only one bird. *Courtesy of The French Corner.*

Wonderful and rare teapot with raised oriental design, different on each side, 5" tall. *Courtesy of The French Corner.* $650-750.

The other side of the teapot has a different landscape. *Courtesy of The French Corner.*

Laundry set with floral design, *savon* for soap, *sable* for sand, and *soude* for soda. *Courtesy of The French Corner.* $350-380.

"JAPY" kitchen set with floral design. *Courtesy of The French Corner.* $1,900-2,200 for set.

"End of the day" irrigator with color combination consisting of dark and light blue, white, and pink. *Courtesy of The French Corner.* $220-250.

Detail of the floral design on the kitchen set. *Courtesy of The French Corner.*

115

Very rare and popular droopy check canister set, six pieces in excellent condition. *Courtesy of The French Corner.* $1,100-1,200 for set.

The famous big checkered design, but in blue. *Courtesy of The French Corner.* $320-380.

Nice red with blue raised check design for this hanger. *Courtesy of The French Corner.* $280-350.

Orange droopy check hanger. *Courtesy of The French Corner.* $450-560.

Rare lid with hand painted oriental design, riveted knob, from Belgium, c. 1880. *Courtesy of The French Corner.* $230-260.

Basin with floral design. *Courtesy of The French Corner.* $250-295.

Pretty small coffee pot with partly hand painted bird and flowers, probably German. *Courtesy of The French Corner.* $295-350.

Nice blue background with hand painted flowers and bird, 10" tall. *Courtesy of The French Corner.* 550-595.

Airbrushed floral design on this body pitcher, also exists in other colors such as green, blue, or brown. *Courtesy of The French Corner.* $320-350.

"End of the day" salt box with French lettering. *Courtesy of The French Corner.* $480-550.

"End of the day" body pitcher, riveted.
Courtesy of The French Corner. $680-750.

Other side of the coffee pot below is decorated
only with flowers. Mint condition, very rare quality
piece. *Courtesy of The French Corner.*

Exceptional little coffee pot, abundantly decorated with
raised floral design and butterfly on the main side,
fastened spout and riveted, 8" tall. *Courtesy of The French
Corner.* $650-750.

Coffee pot with unusual check design and colors, DUCO, Czechoslovakia. *Courtesy of The French Corner.* $260-295.

Interesting coloring for this coffee pot with filter, signed "DUCO." *Courtesy of The French Corner.* $295-320.

Kitchen utensil rack with yellow and red geometric design, SAINT-SERVAIS, Belgium. Courtesy of The French Corner. $240-260.

Canister set with rare coloring, origin DUCO. Courtesy of The French Corner. $680-750.

Very nice body pitcher with raised Art Deco design, rare yellow background. *Courtesy of The French Corner.* $595-680.

Exceptional butter dish with raised floral design, brown background, The brown gives a wonderful intensity to the other colors. *Courtesy of The French Corner.* $280-350.

"End of the day" glasses drainer, riveted. *Courtesy of The French Corner.* $695-780.

Complete coffee pot with raised floral design. *Courtesy of The French Corner.* $595-670.

Wonderful toilette set, complete and hand painted.
Courtesy of The French Corner. $1,280-1,450.

Detail of the floral design. *Courtesy of The French Corner.*

This view shows the other side of the
pitcher. *Courtesy of The French Corner.*

Detail of the soap box. *Courtesy of The French Corner.*

Light blue coffee biggin with raised roses, 16"
tall. *Courtesy of The French Corner.* $680-750.

Detail of the raised floral design on the beautiful
body pitcher below. *Courtesy of The French
Corner.*

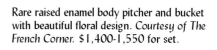

Rare raised enamel body pitcher and bucket
with beautiful floral design. *Courtesy of The
French Corner.* $1,400-1,550 for set.

Chapter Six

Buying and Pricing

As collectors, we always recommend that you learn about enameled ware and educate your eyes before buying. Do not hesitate to speak with specialized dealers, who will always be happy to share their passion with you. Learn about the various time periods so you will know which pieces you prefer and how to recognize them. The more knowledgeable you are, the more you will be able to find the most wonderful pieces at bargain prices, even if price is not the main issue. A specialized dealer will certainly price his treasures at a more justified value, based on knowing what is exceptional or not and disregarding the tremendous increase in the popularity of enameled ware during the last ten years.

There are several points to keep in mind concerning the value of enameled ware pieces. Do not forget that enameled ware is rare, especially complete pieces, and therefore the temptation of replacing a lid with another on a coffee pot or a canister is big. Incomplete pieces have little value and can only be used as decorations. This is why knowledge is important.

Both the lids and the filters must be originals; the best way to check for this is to know that on the lids there is always a detail that reminds you of the main decoration. The detail can be a simple line or a flower motif, but a decorated piece never has a plain lid. On coffee biggins, the filters are always decorated like the main body; the other filters without handles often have a simple gold line.

Do not buy pieces that have been repainted or that are damaged in a very visible place, like in the middle of the main decoration. Damage is acceptable on edges, handles, and lids if not too significant and located in a place where you do not spot it immediately. The same is true of the decoration, which should be fresh and shining. A piece that has been used too much is less valuable.

Pieces with holes are acceptable, especially if found on the oldest items and if the holes are not too big. Repairs like old welding are sometimes found and are also acceptable.

Of course, as with any other collected items, the more intact and well preserved a piece is, the higher its value will be. You might find the same model several times, but never in the same condition. Do not forget that enameled ware was originally used on a daily basis and that while enamel does not break, it does chip. Given that pieces were used over and over again, this makes undamaged items very rare; a piece in perfect condition will always be more expensive. Recently, more pieces that have been professionally restored are being found on the market. Those restorations using enamel instead of paint are very difficult to detect when well done and are acceptable if the restorations are minor.

Other factors influencing price include colors, designs, and origin. In certain countries, people collect more pieces from a certain factory, like Japy-Frères in France or the very famous blue stripes with garlands of roses from B&B. The large white and red checkered motif is also very popular. The most important factor is of course the age – the older a piece is, the more rare and unique it is. Often, people start their collection with a very simple piece and move slowly towards those wonderful jewels that date from the nineteenth century.

Prices on the market change quickly but a certain range can be estimated depending on the chosen items. A decorated coffee pot, for example, can vary from $200 to $1800 for exceptional pieces; a salt box from $150 to $550; a match box from $180 to $350; a canister set from $350 to over $1000; a body pitcher from $120 to over $1000; and utensil racks from $100 to $650. Of course, these are all just approximations, as when you search for enameled ware, like everything else in the antique world, you can find everything from very inexpensive pieces to the most expensive pieces – the choice is yours!

Extremely rare, wonderful canister set, complete, signed "ETOILE," Belgium, red with raised enamel floral design. *Courtesy of The French Corner.* $1,800-1,950.

Detail of flowers on this exceptional canister set. *Courtesy of The French Corner.*

Coffee pot with the same design, rare. *Courtesy of The French Corner.* $380-420.

Rare red marbled body pitcher, 18" tall.
Courtesy of The French Corner. $520-580.

Complete kitchen utensil rack, never used, still has "JAPY" paper label on the front. Beautiful red marbled design. *Courtesy of The French Corner.* $380-420.

Belgian set, "SAINT-SERVAIS," unusual coloring. *Courtesy of The French Corner.* Canister set $520-580, coffee pot $380-420, match box $250-280, salt box $280-320, hanger $240-260.

Lovely coffee pot with roses and pansies. *Courtesy of The French Corner.* $295-350.

Unusual blue shading with roses on this coffee biggin. *Courtesy of The French Corner.* $420-520.

Rare set with elegant floral design, riveted, original bamboo handle. *Courtesy of The French Corner.* $850-950 for set.

Detail of this wonderful design. *Courtesy of The French Corner.*

Matching water pitcher, bamboo handle. *Courtesy of The French Corner.* $350-380.

Body pitcher with white and blue shading, floral design,
"JAPY," France. *Courtesy of The French Corner.* $550-585.

Rare raised floral design on this coffee biggin. *Courtesy of The French
Corner.* $620-670.

Wonderful coffee pot, complete and riveted, very elegant raised
floral design. *Courtesy of The French Corner.* $580-650.

Charming small pitcher with flowers.
Courtesy of The French Corner. $220-250.

Coffee biggin with red shading effect, raised flowers
and bird. *Courtesy of The French Corner.* $780-850.

Raised enamel coffee biggin with bird and flowers. *Courtesy of The French*
Corner. $780-850.

Rare toilette set, basin, pitcher, comb box and
soap box in mint condition. *Courtesy of The
French Corner.* $1,200-1,400.

Detail of the soap box. *Courtesy of The French Corner.*

Detail of the water pitcher, charming floral
design. *Courtesy of The French Corner.*

Matching coffee biggin, same design.
Courtesy of The French Corner. $620-680.

Detail of the comb box. *Courtesy of The
French Corner.*

Coffee pot with filter, raised floral design. *Courtesy of The French Corner.* $580-660.

"JAPY" salt box, very sophisticated floral design with green shading. *Courtesy of The French Corner.* $380-450.

Very elegant and rare pitcher, decorated with hand painted flowers, bird in a nest, c. 1880. *Courtesy of The French Corner.* $480-550.

Beautiful coffee biggin with hand painted landscape on pink shading. *Courtesy of The French Corner.* $580-650.

Rare color and rare floral design on this coffee biggin. *Courtesy of The French Corner.* $580-650.

Set of body pitchers, blue, green, and floral. *Courtesy of The French Corner.* From $160 to 550.

Wonderful teapot with unusual background, designed with raised flowers. *Courtesy of The French Corner.* $520-590.

Large coffee biggin, green background with raised floral design, 14" tall. *Courtesy of The French corner.* $480-560.

Complete coffee pot with wonderful raised flowers, rare piece. *Courtesy of The French Corner.* $580-660.

Unique and exceptional hand painted cake plate, highly collectible piece decorated with bird, flowers, and insect, c. 1850. *Courtesy of The French Corner.* $950-1,100.

Wonderful pitcher with lid, oriental décor, typical of c. 1880. *Courtesy of The French Corner.* $580-650.

Art Nouveau umbrella stand, floral design, partly hand painted, 24" tall. *Courtesy of The French Corner.* $1,100-1,200.

Detail of the handle, very sophisticated and elegant design. *Courtesy of The French Corner.*

Beautiful coffee pot from Belgium, flowers and butterfly design, c. 1885. *Courtesy of The French Corner.* $650-690.

The very rare shape of this partly hand painted coffee pot makes this piece unique. *Courtesy of The French Corner.* $495-560.

Body pitcher with hand painted flowers. *Courtesy of The French Corner.* $380-420.

One of the most collectible designs: flowers and birds. This coffee pot has a bird trying to catch a butterfly. *Courtesy of The French Corner.* $750-800.

Coffee biggin in raised enamel with floral design and bird. Rare piece, 12" tall. *Courtesy of The French Corner.* $790-860.

Detail of this beautiful bird. It is interesting to see how the painter was playing with colors. *Courtesy of The French Corner.*

Wonderful "end of the day" body pitcher. *Courtesy of The French Corner.* $750-820.

Rare design, flowers surrounding a landscape with a boat on a lake, raised enamel. *Courtesy of The French Corner.* $580-650.

Hand painted floral design on this coffee pot, fastened spout and riveted. *Courtesy of The French Corner.* $380-450.

Lovely teapot, riveted and partly hand painted. 6" tall. *Courtesy of The French Corner.* $320-360.

Lovely teapot, rare coloring with raised enamel floral design, Germany. *Courtesy of The French Corner.* $480-540.

Coffee pot with an unusual design, the décor continues all around the coffee pot. *Courtesy of The French Corner.* $595-660.

One of the tallest coffee biggins we've ever had, 17" tall, riveted. Raised floral design, an exceptional piece. *Courtesy of The French Corner.* $1,100-1,150.

This exceptional tray is one of the main pieces in our collection. It is rare for many reasons, including age (c. 1850), colors, and quality of painting. *Courtesy of The French Corner.* $1,100-1,200.

Detail of the roses. This work is an example of the level of painting done by those highly qualified workers that we really should call artists. It is work that can be compared to any other in the fine arts. *Courtesy of The French Corner.*

Teapot with raised floral design, riveted 6" tall. *Courtesy of The French Corner.* $550-650.

Very rare canister, *sucre* for sugar in French, raised floral design and riveted knob, c. 1850. *Courtesy of The French Corner.* $395-480.

Flower pot with handles, green shading with landscape, c. 1850. *Courtesy of The French Corner.* $1,200-1,300.

Detail of the landscape, beautiful subject. *Courtesy of The French Corner.*

Sophisticated raised floral design on a complete coffee
pot. *Courtesy of The French Corner.* $580-670.

Charming little creamer, pink with a winter
landscape, 4" tall. *Courtesy of The French
Corner.* $250-295.

Beautiful kettle with hand painted garland of roses. *Courtesy of The French Corner.* $780-820.

Detail of the roses, nice combination of colors. *Courtesy of The French Corner,*

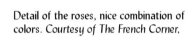

Red chicken wire salt box, unusual background for this design. *Courtesy of The French Corner.* $540-580.

Kitchen utensil rack with lovely Art Deco design. *Courtesy of The French Corner.* $280-320.

"B&B" hanger with blue stripes and garland of roses. *Courtesy of The French Corner.* $340-380.

Another impressive set from "B&B," Austria, with a stylized garland of flowers.
Very charming and elegant design, rare. *Courtesy of The French Corner.*

Canister set, mint condition, French lettering.
Courtesy of The French Corner. $850-950.

Teapot, rare, mint condition. Courtesy
of The French Corner. $450-480.

Coffee pot with filter. Courtesy of
The French Corner. $595-680.

Pitcher with lid, rare and elegant piece. *Courtesy of The French Corner.* $380-450.

Milk carrier. *Courtesy of The French Corner.* $380-420.

Pitcher. *Courtesy of The French Corner,* $350-380.

Footed colander. *Courtesy of The French Corner.* $280-350.

Pan and set of dishes. *Courtesy of The French Corner.* Tall pan, $350-380.

Set of five dishes, different sizes, rare article. *Courtesy of The French Corner.* $900-960 for set.

The three essential wall hung items. *Courtesy of The French Corner.* Match box, $450-520, kitchen utensil rack $280-350, salt box $420-480.

Set of pans with lids. *Courtesy of The French Corner.* $1,200-1,400 for set.

Wall-hung colander and two oven pans. *Courtesy of The French Corner.* Colander $260-280, pans 180-220 each.

Conclusion

After ten years of enameled ware being the center of what is called the "country French style" so in vogue, it was time for enameled ware to be recognized and respected by the antique world as valuable in and of itself – it was time to protect these pieces against ignorance. Now that the market is more stable and realistic, the right value is given to the right object.

This general recognition of French enameled ware was also necessary because the market is constantly in evolution and because the stock of French enameled ware has become more and more limited. Much of it is so rare that in order to respond to the demand, the market is importing pieces in raised enamel from other origins, like Pakistan and India, using different criteria with regard to age (i.e., whether old or not), esthetics, and design.

But it is still a wonderful time to collect, and perhaps inspiration or your own destiny will play a role in starting or adding to your collection. In our case, Yves inherited some pieces of enameled ware when his grandmother passed away, and by trying to find matching pieces we discovered how huge and wonderful this world was.

Perhaps someone will share his or her love of enameled ware with *you*, and if so, you too will be touched by the charm of these beautiful witnesses to the past.

Lovely large hanger, hand painted with landscape and birds, Art Nouveau style. *Courtesy of The French Corner.* $350-420.

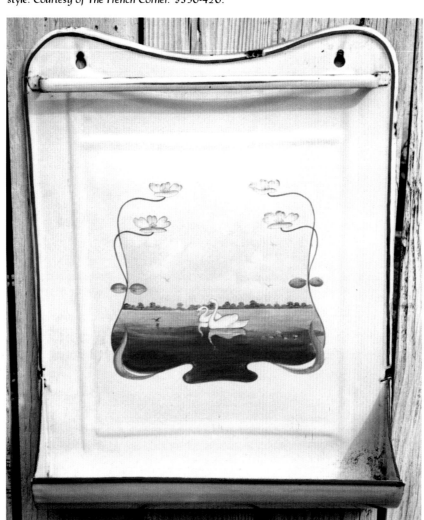

Bibliography

Books

Cabré, Monique. *Dans la cuisine: Objets du désir*. Paragon Editions, 2000.

Greguire, Helen. *The Collector's Encyclopedia of Granite Ware*. Paducah, Kentucky: Collector Books, 1990.

Greguire, Helen. *The Collector's Encyclopedia of Granite Ware Book II*. Paducah, Kentucky: Collector Books, 1993.

Mouret, Jean-Noél. *Les Cuisines de nos grands-mères*. Hatier, 1995.

Queiilier-Guillois, Véronique. *La Cafetière de ma Grand-Mère*. Véronique Queiilier-Guillois Editions, 2002.

Ten Kate-Von Eicken, Brigitte. *L'Émail dans la Maison*. Armand Colin Editions, 1992.

Brochures

La Vie en Émaillé. Musée de la Vie Wallonne à Liège, 1993.

Mossiat, Anne. *La Casserole: La Vie en Émaillé à Saint-Servais*. Musée des Arts Anciens du Namurois, 1994.

Periodicals

Cabrè, Monique. "A la cuisine, les ustensiles créent le décor." *Aladin*, March 1999.

Faveton, Pierre. "Tôle à perpétuité." *Art et décoration*, January/February, 1999.

"French Enamelware." *Country Living*, February, 1999.

"L'Émail dans la Cuisine." *Antiquités Brocante*, March, 2001.

"Ustensiles de Cuisine en émail." *La Vie due Collectionneur*, No 293, Novembre, 1999.

Zamboni, Agnès. "Émail d'antan." *Campagne Décoration*, No 13, January/February, 2002.

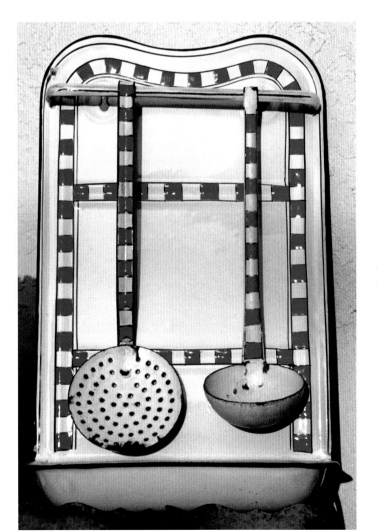

Complete kitchen utensil rack with red check design. *Courtesy of The French Corner.* $350-360.